rise

Rashika Perera Gomez

Copyright © 2019 Rashika Perera Gomez

All rights reserved. No part of this book may be reproduced in any form or by any electronic or mechanical means, including information storage and retrieval systems, without permission in writing from the publisher, except by reviewers, who may quote brief passages in a review.

Paperback ISBN 978-06485774-0-9
Hardcover ISBN 9780-6485774-1-6

Front cover and book design by Roshanee Rebera.

Printed by IngramSpark.

First printing edition 2019.

riseprintmedia@gmail.com
https://riseprintmedia.wixsite.com/rashikapereragomez

Dedicated to my precious daughters

It is because of you that I RISE.

Dedicated to my family and friends

You helped me RISE.

Acknowledgments

Writing this book was a journey.

I am ever so grateful to my tribe for inspiring, helping, pushing, and pulling me, every step of the way. Thank you to my first "publisher," my father, Rajitha Perera, who patiently compiled all my writings while I was in high school and university, giving me a taste of what it felt like to write a "book." Thank you for the many promptings from family and friends to "write a book"! I listened to you. Thank you to my supportive and talented family: my mother, Maheshini Perera, sister, Savindri Perera, aunts Roshanee Rebera and Dhilanthi Fernando, and uncle Noel Rebera. Thank you for scouring these pages, editing, fine tuning, and polishing my writing. Thank you to my designer Roshanee Rebera. I am grateful for the countless hours you spent making this book beautiful and for turning my vision to reality. Thank you "life" for the many lessons you have served me. Thank you to my fellow travellers who trusted me with their life stories and life lessons. Our stories made this book.

As I watched the sun set on that fateful day, I knew I would never see that sunset again. I knew that nothing will ever be the same.

Everything was about to change. It was petrifying, yet electrifying.

As I drove away from my old life, tears streamed down my face.

Tears of sadness for what I had lost.
Tears of defeat knowing that all my effort had been in vain.
Tears of pain for the hurt I had endured.
Tears of fear for all the unknowns ahead.
Tears of relief that the weight on my shoulders was lifted.
Tears of joy for what was to come.
Tears.
Many tears.

My new life arrived with full force. It was a shocker of a year, with intense highs and treacherous lows. And yet through it all, the sun set and rose, every single day.

Life went on.
I survived.
I thrived.

It was the year to break me. It was the year to make me. I discovered that life is not about the destination, it's about the beauty of every single moment. I learned that I love life, even the ugly, painful bits.

For that ugliness masks the beauty in the pain. Life's precious gems often come to us in our darkest, hardest, and most crushing of hours. This is true for me, and this is true of almost every single person who sits on my therapy couch. As a psychologist, I have had the enormous honour of journeying with others on the rollercoaster called life…traversing with them as they navigate motherhood, relationships, transitions and so much more. There are many thieves who steal our peace of mind. It could be a partner, it could be friends or family, it could be illness, it could be a job. These thieves try to sink us. We choose how we respond.

This collection of poems is our story. And for us all, while the sun sets, it also rises.

Rashika

Contents

I Will Rise	2
365	4
Mother	6
There For You	7
L . O . V. E.	9
Super Woman	12
They Watch, They Learn	14
Living	16
Are You Ok?	18
The Mask	19
Click	22
Love Me	24
Be You	26
Words	28
Cry	30
Mirror Mirror	32
This is Me	34
Lost	36
Soar	38
The Sisterhood	40
Take Time	42
Seasons	43

The Art of Letting Go	46
Anger	48
You	50
Love Yourself	52
Listen	54
No Lock, No Key	56
Door	58
You Can	60
Home	62
I am Not Yours	64
The Last Time	66
Wish Them Well	67
Let Them	69
You Will Never Know	72
Walk	74
Kaleidoscope	76
Pearl	78
Dance!	80
Shreds	82
The Lover	84
Bud	86
Rise!	88

I Will Rise

You step on a flower, it releases perfume
You crush sandalwood, it releases its aromas
You boil a tea bag, it releases its flavours
You stress out a muscle, it releases strength
You cage a caterpillar, it releases a butterfly
You kill a phoenix, it releases a new life

You beat me down. It releases me.
I. Will. Rise.

365

In 365 days
A lot can happen
As life sends you on a rollercoaster ride
You experience the highs and lows
The curve balls it throws
You either crumble and stumble
Or survive and thrive
And the things that ground you, that ensure you grow are
Family
Friends...true friends
Faith
Love
Courage
Resilience
Hope
As you grow a year older
Experiencing beginnings and endings
You may close chapters that pull you back
And open ones that spring you forward
You are not the same 'you' you were 365 days ago
And that's ok
Change is inevitable
Change can be good
Life shapes, refines, and builds you
And you become a different 'you' each day

Mother

When you see a mother, you see a woman who has endured much
A woman who nurtured two tiny cells into a baby
A woman who experienced all her organs shifting, to make room for the new tenant
A woman who sacrificed how she ate, slept, dressed, lived, to give her child all of her
A woman who gave up or postponed her dreams, to help her child dream their own dreams
A woman who was often tired
A woman who was courageous even when every fibre of her was shaking
A woman who kept going because little eyes were watching her
When you see a mother, you see a wonder woman

There For You

When you were the size of a sesame seed...
I was there for you
When you entered this world and let out your first cry...
I was there for you
When you looked for comfort in this new scary world...
I was there for you
When you took your first step...
I was there for you
When you had your first fall...
I was there for you
When you are upset that the banana is opened the wrong way...
I am here for you
When your sister grabs your dolly and it's the end of the world...
I am here for you
When that kid in the playground pushes you and you are sad...
I am here for you
When you are scared to walk into the "big children" school for the first time...
I will be there for you
When you experience your first heartache...
I will be there for you

When it's no longer cool to have mum in your life...
I will be there for you
When you go through life's ups and downs...
I will be there for you
And hopefully, when I am not there, all those times I have been there will help you feel like I am still there for you
But more than that, I hope you realise that all along,
YOU have been there for me too

L . O . V. E.

Love is carrying you for nine months
Love is the scar across my belly that will never go away
Love is waking up several times a night, every single night, for years
Love is missing meals so you can have thirty minutes more of uninterrupted sleep on my lap
Love is cold coffee...every. single. day.
Love is skipping showers
Love is going to the toilet with a miniature audience
Love is tending to you when my head is throbbing from a migraine and my entire body hurts
Love is going to the shops to buy something for myself, and coming home instead with five bags of goodies for you
Love is stifling my smile when you are genuinely distressed that your cracker is broken and showing you empathy instead
Love is holding you when you chuck a tantrum instead of wanting you to just snap out of it
Love is loving you when you "don't like" me for depriving you of a cookie
Love is loving the things you love
Love is genuinely being happy in your moments of joy
Love is giving when you feel like you have nothing to give
Love is hard work
Love is unconditional
Love is behind the scenes

Love is the boring things
Love hurts
Love is joyful
Love is patient
Love is kind
Love sacrifices
Love does not wait for reward
Love is given, even when it isn't always returned
Love is persistent, against all odds
Love is knowing my heart no longer lives with me...it lives in you
Love is, my darling angels
Love. just. is.

Super Woman

She gets up before dawn
And sleeps past midnight
Every single day is a struggle and a fight
To keep life simple, secure, and warm
For her little babies who are in the midst of a thundering storm

As the war rages around she keeps her feet planted
She works hard to fulfil everything that's wanted
By her babies to feel loved, happy, light, and free
To protect them from sadness and misery

Her energy is stretched thin and black circles line her eyes
Her pockets are near empty as she carefully buys
Food to feed her children and clothes and books and toys
Ignoring her own needs and wants for the sake of her children's joys

But her heart is full of love and her life is very rich
She smiles as she watches her babies in their sleep twitch
Her reward comes in the form of kisses and smiles
For these angels she would walk a million miles

A single mother is in a league of her own
She is judged by many, even scorned by some
She possesses courage, pain, and strength like no other
So please be kind when you meet such a mother

They Watch, They Learn

They watch, they learn

You heal and kiss their little scuffs and bruised knees, they become healers

You love and embrace others, they learn to love large

You cook, clean, and work hard, they learn to be responsible

You tend to them, they tend to their dolls…and others

You show kindness to others, they become kind

You sing, they sing

You shout, they shout

You live a life of anger, they learn to hold on to anger

You lie, they learn to become deceptive

They are watching you.

All the time.

What do you want them to learn from you?

Living

I tried
Every single day
With every breath I took
To be "better," "more" of this and "less" of that
And as I tried to be all these things
I lost
Me

I still kept trying
Hoping that all my efforts would amount to something, anything, everything
But
It never did
And so I stopped
'Cos every day I tried, a part of me died

I stopped trying...I stopped dying
I started living

Are You Ok?

You seemed ok
So I didn't ask a thing
You smiled a lot
And with your heart you did sing
You beamed in photos
So no one could tell
That beneath that great exterior
It wasn't all well
Facebook portrayed a life that was merry
It masked a soul and heart that was heavy
You helped others find joy and eased their pain
In the meantime you cried so many tears in vain
If you know someone who is "happy," funny," or "strong"
Don't assume that in their lives nothing is wrong
Just as much as they care for others, they need care too
So stop to ask them, "How are you?"

The Mask

It isn't always as it seems
There can be pain beneath a face that beams
The "strong" hide cracks we cannot see
It isn't as perfect as it appears to be

A smiling face may hide the tears
That have brewed for years and years
Beneath the jokes there could be scars
That have made them cry for hours and hours

The "strong" could be weak and vulnerable too
They may not know what on earth to do
Beneath their self-assured confident ways
Could be a soul whose heart achingly prays

Those smiling eyes, jokes, and wit
Those brilliant people who never seem to quit
Those with the picket fence, the Merc, the lot
Those who cross their "t"s and "i"s they dot

They may be yearning for you to notice their pain
They may be scared to reach out, so they refrain
Look at people in your life and really see
Whether all is well as it should be

Offer the question "How do you do?"
Be curious and ask, "What's going on with you?"
The answer lies not always in what they say
But how they say it and what they don't say

"Strong" people have cracks too, remember this
They maybe there for others when their own lives aren't bliss
One day they may grow tired of the blows with which they've been hit
So reach out to them before they quit

Click

Happy moments
Captured
Cropped
Filtered
Uploaded
Monitored for "likes," "loves," "hahas," and "wows"
We gape at others' lives
Everyone eating amazing food
Seeing amazing sunsets
Travelling to exotic places
Doing adventurous things
Having the time of their life
And so so happy
Everyone…except you…or so you think…
We sometimes only see the happiness reel
Not what people truly feel
Not what is actually happening each day
When things are not so happy and gay
No one lives a perfect life
We all have pain, we all have strife
In between those happy clicks life ticks…sometimes unspectacular, sad, ugly, pathetic, unbearable, imperfect
So don't judge others or yourself by the highlights shown
Life isn't one amazing photo after another
Life is what happens between the photos

Love Me

Love me when I'm beautiful
Love me when I'm worn
Love me when the entire world just looks at me with scorn
Love me when I'm tired
Love me when I'm flying
Love me when the entire world has stopped even trying

Love me tomorrow
Love me today
Love me in every humanly possible way
Love me when I'm difficult
Love me when I'm nice
Love me when things aren't just sugar and spice

Love me when you hate me
Love me when I hate you
Love me when I lose my way and don't know what to do
Love me, don't use me
Love me, don't lose me
Love me, choose me

Please
Just love me

Be You

You are not oversensitive…you have feelings
You are not weak…you are kind
You are not a pushover…you are forgiving
You are not a "big woman"…you are assertive…and happen to be a woman
You are not too vocal…you are articulate
You are not dumb…you are intelligent
You are not emotional…you have emotions
You are not opinionated…you have opinions
You are not ugly…you are beautiful…in every single way
You are not useless…you are worthy and wonderful
You are not who they say you are…you are who you believe in your heart to be
Don't let others define "you"
Be you

Words

They can soothe, they can arouse
They can heal, they can hurt
They can build up, they can tear down
They can inspire, they can discourage
They can breathe life, they can summon death
They can be sweet, they can be dark
They can speak the truth, they can lie
They can defend, they can attack
They can create, they can destroy
They can trigger peace, they can trigger war
They can evoke joy, they can evoke pain
They can appreciate, they can take for granted
They can free, they can imprison
They can make, they can break
They can love, they can hate
Words
They matter
They have power
They have energy
Words
Choose them well

Cry

They cascade
Down the cheeks
Spring forth at nothing
When does it stop?
The hurt brims
Even as the heart sings
So confusing
Can the heart be so happy and so sad at the same time?
The tears stream from a bottomless pit...
Or so it seems
The water helps
Don't stop it
It soothes
It calms
It heals
It cools the hot, searing pain
And before you know it
One day
Those tears will run dry
So
Cry

Mirror Mirror

Look in the mirror, who do you see?
Who is staring back, is it really me?

My image had been defined by the world and you
I sometimes forget what is really true

You are "this," you are "that," we are often told
"Too sensitive," "too cold," "too young," "too old"

Others hold their mirrors up to show me who I am
To shape me and mould me, tell me what I can't and can

My inner voice goes quiet, drowned out by the world
I lose sight of the person behind the girl

One day the mirror cracks, I am lost and confused
For others' needs my image was used

I slowly rebuild my own version of me
I care no more what others can see

The mirror I hold now is my very own
I see in the mirror a girl who has grown

Mirror mirror on the wall
I know myself and I own my all

This is Me

I am not perfect
But I am perfectly imperfect
My vulnerabilities make me soft
My strengths make me formidable
My trials make me wise
My wins make me rise
Life breaks me
Life makes me
And what you see…this is me

Lost

Shake shake shake
Everything spins
All that you know...gone
All comfort stripped away
Shaken to the core
Where do you belong?
Who are you?
What do you do?
The questions only cause more fear
When you are stripped to nothing
You stop caring
...about pleasing everyone
...about what everyone thinks
...about the laws that governed you
You start befriending your inner world
Learning what is left when all is lost
What has endured the fiercest fire
You learn what matters
You learn who matters
You learn who you are
You lose yourself, only to find yourself

Soar

It got heavy
That mask she wore
It got tiring
The pain she bore

And then came the release
She did not have to endure anymore

She dropped the facade
She revealed her core
She surrounded herself
With people she did adore
She rid her life
of things that brought her woe
She learned very quickly
Who was her friend and foe

And finally she did SOAR!

The Sisterhood

She is tough
Yet tears roll down her cheeks often
She works hard from morning to bedtime and beyond
Yet every inch of her feels burnt out
She is brave and scared
Happy and sad
Strong and soft
Firm and kind
Fierce and gentle
Funny and serious
Wise yet capable of questionable choices
A collection of complexity and contradictions
She endures the judgement of the world
Yet she carries on, no apologies for her life and decisions
Living, learning, evolving
Embracing with passion the one life she has been given
She is amazing
She is the sisterhood around me
She is you
She is me

Take Time

Take time to kiss your loved ones
Take time to smell and taste your coffee
Take time to sniff your baby
Take time to chit-chat with the checkout lady
Take time to say thank you, even for the small things
Take time to look up from your phone and smile with someone
Take time to observe a toddler play
Take time to get lost in the music you love
Take time to breathe...slowly and intentionally
Take time to look at your loved ones...and actually see them
Take time to smell the earth after the rain
Take time to soak in the sunshine
Take time to look at the rainbow
Take time to smell the roses...really...not just a cliché
Take time to say "I love you"
Take time to do the things that matter and give you and others joy
Time waits for no one
Don't run out of time and leave room for regrets
Take time

Seasons

We wait
Often impatiently
Wishing for, wanting, craving, needing 'something else'

We watch the clock
Endless tick-tocks
Frustration, sadness, confusion welling within our restless hearts
When will change come?
Will it ever come?

The seconds don't go any faster
The seed doesn't sprout any sooner
The sun doesn't rise any quicker
Winter doesn't end any earlier
For all these things there is a set time

And so it is for the moments and seasons of our lives
They come when they come
Not a moment too early
Not a moment too late

So, how shall we wait?
We can wait
Impatiently
Angrily
Sadly
Desperately
And miss all the seconds ticking by
Or
We can wait 'well'
Finding beauty in the winter
Until the snow melts away

The Art of Letting Go

Hold a feather, it is light
For the smallest wind, it takes flight

Keep holding that feather, five minutes more,
It now weighs more than it did before

Still holding on a few hours later
The strain on my fingers is becoming greater

A whole day later my arm is laden
My fingers frozen, beneath this burden

This 'light' feather is light no more
Oh if only I had let it go

Our hurts, grudges, problems, big and small
We grip them tightly, grip them all

They weigh us down, they ruin our day
So let the cool winds blow them away!

Anger

It consumed me
Because
You used me
You abused me
You lied
You saw me cry
You saw me slowly die
And you did nothing to help me
Instead
You tried harder to destroy me
My anger grew
How could you?
The anger hurt me
The anger burnt me
The anger tired me
The anger changed me
This was not about you anymore
It was about me
My anger served no one
My anger only connected me to you
And I didn't want you in my life anymore
So
I let my anger go

You

You
Are
Worthy

"You" aren't defined by others'
Words
Opinions
Perceptions
Misconceptions
Of you

Embrace yourself…all of you
Let no one tell you that you aren't enough
You are
Let no one take your light away
Shine on

Laugh, cry, dream, be silly, be serious, work hard, relax hard
Know yourself
Stand for your truth
You have one life
Live it true to who you are
No apologies
No facades

Live freely
Live fully
Live

Love Yourself

For years I didn't leave
Because
I loved you

One day I finally left
Because
I started loving me

Listen

the still small voice says
no
not now
this isn't right
i don't like it
don't do it
stop
walk away
i am uncomfortable
this is wrong
i hate this
why?
how can you?
say something
i don't deserve this
and
we just don't listen
we silence this voice
time after time after time after time
until the voice screams
life screams
and then
you hear it
do not ignore that voice within
it knows you well
it knows you inside out
listen
to your still...small...voice

No Lock, No Key

I can see the gate, it has no lock, no key
I have a choice to stay or flee

Yet as I reach that gate, my heart pounds
I have gotten accustomed to my cruel surrounds

"Just push the gate!" my head yells
"Just wait a moment…" my heart tells

Many steps to that gate and back
To push that gate the strength I lack

Until one day the camel's back broke
"It is time" my heart quietly spoke

I pushed the gate and stepped outside
Gingerly at first and then full stride

I chose my freedom and chose my fate
To do this in life, it is never too late

Relationships, jobs, insecurities great and small
These can imprison us far more than a wall

Almost always there is a way out
If only we can wade through our fear and doubt

Push. The. Gate.

Door

Why didn't I leave
I ask myself every day
There were not many reasons
For me to still stay

I seemed to disappoint you
In all things, big and small
I kept picking myself up
After every single fall

I couldn't see very clearly
I was afraid to look
To fix everything around me
I read every blooming book

One day I just froze in time
I couldn't struggle anymore
I packed up my broken heart
And walked out that familiar door

Everyone has a limit
Even the kindest souls on earth
Treasure your loved ones daily
And don't forget their worth

If you take them for granted
They may still decide to stay
But their permanent departure
May only be moments away

You Can

You can say no
You can jump off a ride you don't enjoy
You can stop reading a book you don't like
You can stop singing a song which no longer stirs you
You can leave a home which no longer feels like home
You can leave a city to which you no longer belong
You can quit the job you hate
You can ditch your toxic friends who drag you down
You can leave a relationship which robs your soul
You can, you can, you can!
Leaving is not always defeat
Leaving is courageous
Leaving gives you another chance to live the life you want
You CAN leave

You Can

You can say no
You can jump off a ride you don't enjoy
You can stop reading a book you don't like
You can stop singing a song which no longer stirs you
You can leave a home which no longer feels like home
You can leave a city to which you no longer belong
You can quit the job you hate
You can ditch your toxic friends who drag you down
You can leave a relationship which robs your soul
You can, you can, you can!
Leaving is not always defeat
Leaving is courageous
Leaving gives you another chance to live the life you want
You CAN leave

Home

Home is
comfort
contentment
joy
peace
laughter
love
fun
kindness
forgiveness
chaos
mess
creativity
openness
play
work
sharing
caring
security
warmth
family
hope
freedom freedom freedom
Home is where you can be all of you
If it isn't these things
It isn't home
Find your home

I am Not Yours

You can smear my name
But you can't take away my character
You can take away my mementos
But you can't take away my memories
You can take my past
But you can't take my future
You can take away my loved ones
But you can't take away our love
You can take away my piano
But you can't take away my music
You can have a lot
But
You
Can't
Have
Me

The Last Time

There will be a last
Cuddle
Kiss
Fight
Look
Smile
Laugh
Tear
Photo
Coffee
Song
Meal
Conversation
Intimate moment
Sunrise
Sunset
One day…it will be the last time

Wish Them Well

Those who lied and marred your name
Those who tried to bring you shame
Wish them well

Those who spat right in your face
Those who chose to question your place
Wish them well

Those who robbed you of happiness and joy
Those who treated you like you were a toy
Wish them well

Those who replaced you within a heartbeat
Those who found it so easy to cheat
Wish them well

Those who made your road so hard
Those who your ideals of love and life scarred
Wish them well

All your troubles made you strong
You are exactly where you belong
What you have gone through is no mistake
The trials have left a victor in their wake

So thank those who provided these lessons to you
Those who made you find your version that's true
Life will work out, surely time will tell

So go ahead...
Wish them well

Let Them

Let them
Smear your name
Twist the truth
Discard you
Misunderstand you

Let them
Waste their breath
Stoop low
Show their colours
Display their shallowness

Let them
Play their petty games
Prop each other's wrongs
Revel in their cruelty
Collude against you

Don't let them
Question your worth
Mute your song
Dull your shine
Rob your joy

Don't let them
Shake your foundations
Bully you
Change you
Touch you

Let your heart stay strong
Unwavering
Knowing your truth
Trusting your truth
Being true

Let them live their lives
And you live yours
Untouched
True
Free

You Will Never Know

Do you even know the oceans of tears I cried?
As every living piece within me died?
I wished someone saw the chaos deep inside
And took away the hurt and pain I tried to hide

You will never know the lengths I went to love you
You will never know what I gave up to prove my love was true
You will never know the despair I felt within
You will never know the price I paid for trusting

You will never know the woman I am today
The past has strangely helped me on my way
The ride was bumpy, nasty, and long
But it brought me to the place where I belong

Walk

As you leave the well-trodden path behind, the road under your feet feels
Unfamiliar
Uncomfortable
Even painful
The pebbles turn to rocks
Jagged, rugged, relentless
As you stumble
Tired, beaten, scarred
Every fibre of your being wants to run away
To jump off the road and never jump back on
But you keep going on that hard hard road
Because you are not travelling alone
Because little hopeful eyes are watching and learning from you
Because you know the hard road ends
Because you know that around the corner is your beautiful destiny
Because you know it is always darkest before the dawn
So
You
Just
Keep
Walking, walking, walking

Kaleidoscope

The kaleidoscope turns
Every glittering piece moves
Tumbling, gliding, sliding into place
Once the cylinder turns...everything changes
The old pattern is gone
The pieces that once stood side by side, may not anymore
Yet
The pieces still glisten
Undulled by the turn
Still creating beauty
Still shining
Making new patterns
Making new beauty
Unfazed
And the kaleidoscope keeps on twisting...twisting...twisting
Creating something new with every turn

Pearl

A grain of sand
Caught between two shells
Love, circled by two lovers
Sand, rubbing against the flesh
Constantly challenged
Ever evolving
Ever growing
It emerges victorious
Shiny
Beautiful
Strong
A
Pearl

Dance!

Twisting and twirling
Smiling and leaping
Angels in tutus
With the world in their hands

Moving to the beat
Swaying on their feet
In imperfect synchrony
Yet happy as can be

Dance
For a chance
To move
To let go
To feel joy
To be free

Shreds

The glass shatters
A million pieces
The dream is lost
The fragments glisten
They are never to be whole again
Yet the pieces come back together
One by one
Not as before, but still beautiful, if not more
A mosaic
Shreds side by side
Its parts differently placed
Broken
Yet somehow
Whole

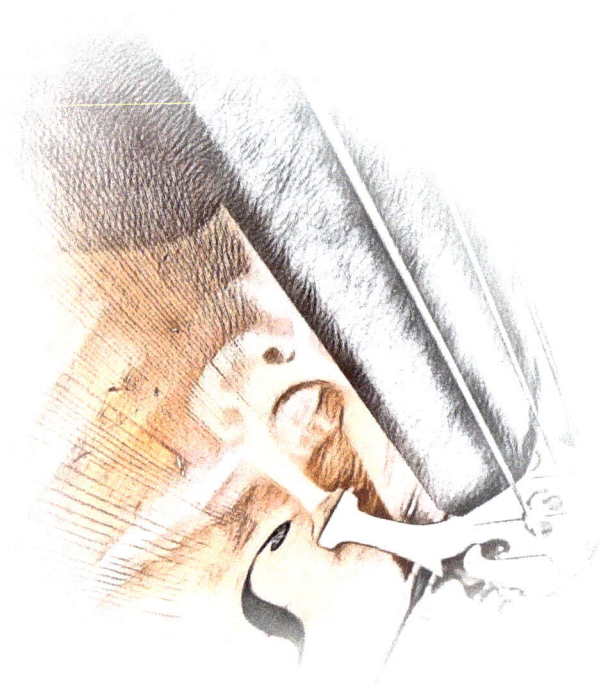

The Lover

She lies silent
Dormant
Waiting
Yearning
Her heart aching for the tender, familiar, caress
Fingers running up and down her spine
Joy spilling out of her every pore
But there is no joy
Only deafening silence
Surely a love so strong will survive
Isn't true love meant to be?
Her lover returns
Battered by the years of separation
Longing to love again
She is held again
Fingers run up and down her spine again
The familiar caress
Joy emanating
They make music together
Her strings vibrating
The bow singing
Gingerly, tentatively at first
Then stronger, sweeter, familiar, comfortable, lovely
The cello sings…again

Bud

The scorching sun beats down
Unrelenting, burning, torturous
The leaves wilt
Trying unsuccessfully to hide from the hot, angry, giant
The leaf dries, barely hanging on
The hot winds blow
Thunder strikes
The stars align
A recipe for disaster...wind, lightning, heat
The tiny spark escalates
The flames singe everything in their path
Nothing is spared
Everything burnt, tested, purified
The refiner's fire snakes the landscape
Leaving charred skeletons behind
Utter loss, utter devastation, utter nothingness
Life ends
Until
Pop
The little bud rises
Then another
Pop
And another
Pop
Green, young, alive
Rebirth
Life, after death

Rise!

I was standing in a dark dark place
Tears streaming down my face
Feeling empty, defeated, stripped to the bone
My whole world broken, I felt so alone

Then the angels appeared
Who wiped away my tears
Swooped in and carried me
Gave me wings that set me free
Made me smile again
Wiped away the pain
Gave me strength to journey on
Filled my life with joy and song

And so I rise
Up to the skies
You don't realise what matters
Until everything gives way
No matter what life throws at me
A host of angels carry me
And most of all, I know that I am free

I am grateful for the fires I journeyed through
They made me stronger and they made me true
Feeling wiser, victorious, I am now reborn
My world full of beauty, no more all alone!

Image Credits

Cover Aleksandra Smirnova/Adobestock.com
Page 1 Mikhail Bakunovich/Shutterstock.com
Page 3 j.chizhe/Shutterstock.com
Page 5 cienpiesnf/Adobestock.com
Page 10 Ket4up/Shutterstock.com
Page 11 Maheshini Perera
Page 13 Rashika Perera Gomez
Page 17 Crazy nook/Shutterstock.com
Page 20 yukitama/Shutterstock.com
Page 23 KatyArtDesign/Shutterstock.com
Page 29 gorchica/Shutterstock.com
Page 31 ESZAdesign/Shutterstock.com
Page 34 Yuriy Seleznev/Shutterstock.com
Page 37 Antuanetto/Adobestock.com
Page 39 Oksana Kalmykova/Shutterstock.com
Page 41 praphab louilarpprasert/Shutterstock.com
Page 44 Erni/Adobestock.com
Page 45 nanka/Shutterstock.com
Page 47 pavlo s/Shutterstock.com
Page 52 Galyna_P/Shutterstock.com
Page 55 Roshanee Rebera
Page 57 archideaphoto/Adobestock.com
Page 61 Didecs/Shutterstock.com
Page 63 raindrop74/Shutterstock.com
Page 68 Sonja Calovini/Shutterstock.com
Page 73 Savindri Perera
Page 75 Senri7/Adobestock.com
Page 80 Rashika Perera Gomez
Page 81 Rashika Perera Gomez
Page 83 Rashika Perera Gomez
Page 85 Sveta Lagutina/Shutterstock.com
Page 87 Billion Photos/Shutterstock.com

**Dr Rashika Perera Gomez** is a closet poet. For years she has been scribbling poems on bits of paper, napkins, journals, and on her blog. Multiple suggestions to publish her poems have been bashfully brushed aside... until now. While Rashika has sat comfortably with her other "labels" such as woman, daughter, mother, sister, friend, psychologist, and musician, it is through the writing of this book that she has taken ownership of the label that always existed, but was never fully acknowledged...that of "poet."

Her life's journey has taken her from Sri Lanka, the land of her birth, to the USA, the land of her education, to Australia, the land that is now her home. In her poems she weaves together her life stories with the stories of those who have crossed her path on this journey between starkly different lands. She gives voice to the sufferings and tribulations of the heartbroken and the victorious. She writes from a position of strength and vulnerability, making her poems relatable to others' life journeys.

RISE is her debut book, and a tribute to those who rise above the most gruelling of life's curveballs.

www.ingramcontent.com/pod-product-compliance
Lightning Source LLC
Chambersburg PA
CBHW062112290426
44110CB00023B/2793